AUTHENTIC INTERIORS

AUTHENTIC INTERIORS
ROOMS THAT TELL STORIES

PHILIP GORRIVAN

Gibbs Smith

For my mother, Marcelle.
You were, and remain, my biggest fan.
Thinking of you always.

CONTENTS

INTRODUCTION

The cultivated art of storytelling has been integral to the human experience for as long as men and women have walked the earth. Storytelling puts our lives in context. Stories track the rise and fall of civilizations. They chronicle cultural evolution. They carry forward family traditions.

Stories can be inspirational, aspirational, or entertaining. They can soothe distress, elicit a joyful grin, or invigorate a dormant imagination. They evoke infinite emotional responses: love, peace, delight, craving, sadness, amusement, and more.

Stepping inside the Rose Main Reading Room of the public library on New York City's 5th Avenue, with its mile-wide shelves lined with leather-bound books, illustrates the primary way we have to advance stories: The written word. The regimented rows of tables and chairs beckon visitors to sit and consider new volumes in near-monastic quiet, in stark contrast to the frenetic boulevards outside.

But we have infinite other ways to tell stories.

Take, for example, the fifteen-thousand-year-old cave paintings in Lascaux, France, five hundred kilometers south of Paris. The primitive-era artists depicted the earliest domestication of animals—deer, horses, cats, birds, and bulls—by examining the relationships between man and beast, hunter and herd.

Theatrical performances—comedic, dramatic, operatic—spin narratives about everything from a murdered king and his vengeful son in Shakespeare's *Hamlet* to the birth of a nation escaping the tyranny of a different king in Lin-Manuel Miranda's *Hamilton*.

So too, the fashion world serves to document our à la mode sartorial lives. Runways reflect myriad cultural influences, including technological advances, political vagaries, economic fluctuations, and, more currently, morphing gender norms.

With a mattress and plinth covered in an ikat-patterned cotton, this seventeenth-century inlaid Dutch daybed is the perfect perch for an afternoon lost in a best-selling novel. Toss pillows in shades of watermelon and persimmon complement the tobacco-toned walls. The photographs hanging above are part of my client's extensive collection.

"The best rooms have something to say about the people who live in them." —*David Hicks*

That brings me to a simple yet essential declaration from the legendary twentieth-century interior designer David Hicks, who remains one of the most important influences in my work as an interior decorator: "The best rooms have something to say about the people who live in them."

The message? Rooms tell stories too. That idea guides the decisions reflected in the homes I design. And as no two stories are the same, the spaces I create are as individual as the DNA of their inhabitants.

To realize authentic interiors, my work as a designer begins with a series of interviews so that I can discover the many details that comprise my clients' life stories, to find out who they are and how they proceed in the world. It's a bit like researching a biography that will physically appear in the arranged furnishings and finishes just beyond a client's front door—as opposed to on the pages of a book.

A young downtown family with an Amagansett beach house might wish to escape to a quiet, casual space on weekends—a place to unwind and enjoy each other's company away from their frantic weekday lives. And perhaps they will want to entertain weekend guests or host breezy buffet dinners after sun-drenched afternoons in the surf.

In interpreting those wishes, I might suggest a warm-and-cool neutral color scheme to tell that story: muted khaki balanced against the palest-blue gray. It's a color combination that reflects the sand and sea and encourages calm. Washed linen slipcovers, detailed with tape trim and dressmaker details; casually unstructured Roman shades outfitting each window; and guest bedrooms inflected with organic, seaside motifs are all ways to manifest the clients' wishes and the story of their home.

A couple on Park Avenue might envision a home that tells a very different story, one of their combined interests in maximalism, contemporary art, and adventurous globe-trotting. I might choose a vibrant mix of furniture from various periods with diverse cultural pedigrees, pieces with juxtapositional silhouettes, bold geometric patterns, and unexpected colors.

Lacquered walls would reflect the light across a room of provocative canvases in dialog with each other. Objects collected from distant excursions could be featured throughout their rooms. And my imagination might turn to a hand-painted and embroidered wallcovering sheathing the dining room walls to spark excitement and spirited conversation.

In both examples, I reflect on my clients' wishes and aspirations through my aesthetic lens.

As for my aesthetic lens, in addition to David Hicks, whose brazen competency with grand-scaled patterns still astounds me, other well-known designers inform and inspire my work.

The celebrated society decorator Dorothy Draper's redecoration of the Greenbrier hotel in White Sulfur Springs, West Virginia—a master class in the relationships of bold, saturated color—reminds me to be adventurous when mixing hues.

Albert Hadley, widely referred to as the Dean of American Decorating, effortlessly combined traditional pieces with their contemporary counterparts—floral chintz-clad French chairs paired with Lucite tables—in ways that give me license to boldly do the same.

Others include Billy Baldwin and his preternaturally tailored apartments, Francis Elkins's effortless mix of disparate architectural details, Jay Spectre's high-octane 1970s flair, and Mark Hampton's ability to craft perfectly edited rooms punctuated with Anglophile references.

And I continue to learn from my contemporaries, as a design education is only limited by the boundaries of curiosity.

From the first meeting to the installation day, I strive to write the next chapter in my clients' lives as reflected in their singular surroundings. I hope you will see those stories evidenced in the fourteen projects featured on the pages of this book.

That is what brings me joy and is the measure against which I gauge the success of my work—one story at a time.

IN THE CITY

FRESH PERSPECTIVE

ON THE BROOKLYN WATERFRONT

While the distance between the neighborhoods of Manhattan's storied Sutton Place and Brooklyn's hipster-chic DUMBO (an acronym for Down under the Manhattan Bridge Overpass) is a mere six miles, the contrast between them would be difficult to overstate. Aside from both being in New York City, the only thing they share is their proximity to the East River. The former defines quintessential Uptown living; the latter epitomizes Downtown style.

Traditional rooms informed by the surrounding historic architecture exemplify the prevailing decorating zeitgeist on Sutton Place, where author Arthur Miller and his wife Marilyn Monroe, shipping magnate Aristotle Onassis, the legendary Judy Garland, and fashion impresario Bill Blass once resided. The sidewalks are tree-lined and manicured; reservedness and understatement are de rigueur.

Juxtapositionally, in Brooklyn, cobblestone boulevards populated with converted industrial buildings offer stellar views of the Manhattan Bridge—not to mention the picturesque city skyline beyond. The area's residential reinvention attracts downtown denizens to DUMBO's trendy boutiques, restaurants, and galleries, where quirky individualism and creativity are celebrated.

So when my clients—a young, entrepreneurial couple—decided to depart Sutton Place to spend the next chapter of their lives in an expansive loft in DUMBO, a fresh perspective for their new home's design became my challenge. They wished to streamline and simplify—in the best sense of the words. In response, we jettisoned time-honored, traditional silhouettes in favor of pared-back modernity; we worked collaboratively to realize a new home reflective of their fresh start. We adopted the goal of creating "quietly refined" rooms.

In our initial meeting, we agreed that the cityscape beyond the home's oversized windows would be the focal point, celebrating my clients' urban experience as lifelong New Yorkers. To that end, we chose minimalistic roller shades to control the sunlight instead of curtains or fabric

PRECEDING OVERLEAF: With outdoor space at a premium in New York City, this expansive terrace was a significant selling point for my clients as they searched for a new home. To allow the stellar view of the Manhattan Bridge—an icon of the city's industrial design—to take center stage, we chose a palette of warm and cool neutrals for the outdoor furnishings. The Brooklyn Grange created and maintains the garden. **OPPOSITE:** A large-scale collage image of Brigitte Bardot by the contemporary artist Jerome Lucani takes pride of place in the home's dining room. French mid-century silhouettes inspired the custom upholstered chairs; they stand in dialog with a dynamic chandelier by Lindsey Adelman. When lit for an evening meal, the chards of light dance across the dining table's subtle sheen, energizing conversation.

The cityscape beyond the home's oversized windows would be the focal point, celebrating my clients' urban experience as lifelong New Yorkers.

shades so the vistas just beyond the glass take center stage. Further, we decided to draw the color palette for the furnishings from the Manhattan Bridge's industrial elements: concrete footings, steel girders, and twisted cables—all visible from nearly every room.

The crisp white walls recede in the primary seating area, serving as the backdrop to the living room's textured pieces, which include two sofas—one salmon-hued with curved lines, and one more linear, in horizontally striped grays. These complementary pieces reflect my clients' relationship—a devoted yet individualistic couple, together since their high school days. The textiles play off each other beautifully: glove leather, plush velvet, and ribbed ottoman cloth. Together, they serve as an extension of my clients' fashion-forward sartorial style.

A shared love of entertaining also guided our decisions. The spacious kitchen features a ceiling-integrated, restaurant-quality exhaust vent for avid cooks interested in expanding their gastronomic repertoire. The stained-oak kitchen islands provide ample space for prepping meals. An adjacent bar cabinet stands ready for martinis.

My clients expressed a wish for sanctuary in the primary bedroom and adjacent bath. To that end, a curvaceous soaking tub is an antidote to frenetic city living, while the lavishly upholstered bed provides a blissful night's sleep.

With the interiors complete, our focus turned to a graciously scaled outdoor terrace—one of New York real estate's most sought-after luxuries. We worked with a Brooklyn-based landscape firm to create lounging and alfresco dining areas. The hardscaping, interspersed with lush planting, adds a welcome naturalistic element—a private park for my clients to enjoy throughout the warm-weather seasons.

PRECEDING OVERLEAF: Adopting a counterintuitive approach, we decided against hanging art in the apartment's sizable, open-plan living room so that the windows might serve to frame the compelling views of the East River and Manhattan skyline to the west. The etched-glass waterfall table, the only piece of furniture repurposed from the clients' home on Sutton Place, effortlessly floats on a textural carpet from Stark. **OPPOSITE:** A haunting stare, comprised of reflective circles set against a black background, is revealed in a sculptural photographic portrait by artist Matt Colagiuri; the sideboard is reminiscent of a Rubik's Cube, revealing a subtle geometric tension. A glinting metallic lamp, a vintage find, adds a distinct 1970s flare to the tableau.

Structural columns are often considered intrusive, but they can be embraced and celebrated with a shift in perspective. To that end, we commissioned Brazilian graffiti artist João Salomão (aka Pixote) to use the column as a canvas. After interviewing my clients, Salomão created a site-specific work that reflects their relationship, making the space supremely personal. The wall-hung work by the same artist informed the color palette for this media room.

LEFT: A West African Snaka Waka totem dances in the hall between the kitchen and living areas. **ABOVE:** A sumptuous mélange of complementary finishes—Venetian plaster, stained oak, and granite—draws the eye around the chef's kitchen, which has ample storage, so the counters are streamlined when not in use. Gaggenau appliances are integrated within the custom cabinetry, while a low-pile, nubby carpet subliminally delineates the kitchen's footprint.

Taken collectively, this array of vignettes represents a long list of design decisions meant to reflect and express my clients' aspirations for a new episode of life in Brooklyn. When I asked them if they could see themselves back on Sutton Place, they emphatically explained, "Unlike uptown, DUMBO is a neighborhood that fosters interpersonal relationships—we interact with people in a way that's intimate and refreshing. We love it here."

In a departure from the home's more muted hues, saturated plum abounds in the primary bedroom, complemented by accents of teal and vibrant blue. The strict linear pattern in the custom channel-tufted headboard and bed frame references the outside architectural elements. The sloping arms of the adjacent club chair add a counterpoint to the crisp angles.

REINVENTION

ON EAST 64TH STREET

While moving to a new home is the primary reason people hire an interior designer, there are myriad other reasons that spur the decision. The wish for updated silhouettes more in keeping with prevailing trends, the need to refurbish the wear and tear that comes from years of enjoying a space, and a change in relationship status are just a few examples. The latter drove the owner of this expansive Upper East Side home to engage me.

Newly single and ready to reinvent, he asked me to create rooms that reflected his wide-ranging interests, which were underrepresented in the apartment's earlier incarnation. We discussed how his experience as a fashion and fine art photographer and documentary filmmaker might inform our decisions. And having historically favored neutral shades, he yearned to push beyond his comfort zone to realize spaces exuberant with color in fresh and optimistic ways.

Celebrating color is my modus operandi, so my first consideration was the palette for the rooms and furnishings. Here, I took a cue from my client's photographs. With a focus on naturalistic motifs in his work—plants, trees, and flowers—I suggested a synthesizing shade of spring green to greet him as he opened the door to the apartment. It took some convincing, but when rendered in high-gloss lacquer on the walls and ceiling, the space vibrates with joy and sets an uplifting tone for the rest of the home. Instead of a carpet, we opted for dark walnut floors, calling to mind the forest floor, which extend the alfresco imagery.

Having taken that leap of faith into color, we turned our attention to spaces beyond the foyer. And as with any spacious home (in this case, 4,800 square feet), finding ways for the eye to move from room to room is crucial. My solution was to employ a single shade of off-white for the moldings and trims throughout. It's a subtle decorating trick that successfully establishes visual cohesion.

We worked with a team of Eastern European lacquer artisans to realize a glistening finish for the walls and ceiling in the home's airy entryway. A sparse approach allows a biomorphic bronze center hall table to be the focus, purchased through Dessin Fournir. A vintage Italian chandelier adds to the drama after dark. **OVERLEAF:** In the formal living room, a pair of custom sofas in the style of Jean-Michel Frank are covered in a textural epingle velvet, with ample space for guests. Unlined, open-weave curtains allow for ambient light while affording privacy. Several toss pillows and the terra-cotta tufted bench in the foreground add color. Photographs by the homeowner, which flank the windows, enhance the room's symmetry.

PRECEDING OVERLEAF: In this seating area, an arresting portrait (at left) by the French expressionist painter Bernard Lorjou holds court; the two floral photographs (at right) are by the homeowner. Beyond that, the dining room's interior architecture is softened by walls upholstered in jaunty geometric silk. Six powder-blue dining chairs mix with two fretwork head chairs perfectly. A pair of drawings by Graham Nixon hang above the hearth.

RIGHT: Adjacent to the entryway, a diminutive Chanel sofa is upholstered in an apple green linen, with an antique English armchair (left) modernized in similarly hued glove leather. At right, a French wood-framed armchair completes the suite. As a counterpoint, the walls are bathed in muted turquoise, while mid-century chrome-and-glass accents add glamour.

OPPOSITE: In the breakfast nook, replete with cookbook shelves, an awning stripe animates the banquette cushions, while a carved chair stands ready to be pressed into service for guests.
ABOVE: In a departure from the conventional, the kitchen features photographs by the homeowner hung gallery-style. The industrial pot rack is at once charming and functional.

In the library, a custom Beauvais carpet populated with octagons and squares calls to mind the work of the 1970s design legend David Hicks. The flooring's shades of green-gray and off-white are repeated on the painted walls and moldings. A polished gunmetal-and-glass coffee table and two chrome-framed armchairs—all by Karl Springer—extend the vintage reference.

Celebrating color is my modus operandi,
so my first consideration was the palette for
the rooms and furnishings.

With large-scale rooms, creating a sense of intimacy calls for ingenuity. For the dining room, my client asked me to design an embracing space conducive to conversations while enjoying meals with friends and family. To accomplish the task, we upholstered the dining room walls; the fabric is luxurious and absorbs sound, creating an enveloping, cozy feel.

The wood-paneled library, once populated with Anglophile antiques and old-world references, called out for an update, too, and here, I asked my client to take a second leap of faith. I suggested painting the knotty-pine paneling in shades of pale green-gray, set off by the off-white trim and ceiling. To counterbalance and ground the room with ample seating, we chose a 1970s classic Saint Thomas sofa, originally designed by Billy Baldwin, upholstered in rich chocolate brown.

For the primary bedroom, we settled on a restful shade of lavender after my client explained that, for him, purple is a neutral hue, remarking, "I find it incredibly calming." And so, with covering a double-width expanse of windows as my initial focus, I searched for a patterned curtain fabric to scheme the room around. A lavender and white warp-dyed ikat proved the perfect solution, introducing an Indonesian motif referencing my client's extensive travels. The overscale, trompe l'oeil carpet added just the right amount of geometry.

As with every interior design project, accessories are the final consideration. For me, the trick is mixing decorative and functional pieces that feel like they have always been there. We accomplished the task by including pieces my client had collected over his lifetime, so he felt instantly at home in his new space.

On one wall of the primary bedroom, a set of figure drawings hangs above a burled walnut Louis Philippe commode, which is topped by a rare piece of Sainte-Anne marble. Two richly patinated Louis Vuitton cases—both decorative and functional—stylishly complete the tableau.

A custom-designed bed with crisp, masculine lines and detailed with chrome nailheads is the focal point of the expansive, sun-bathed primary bedroom. The three-dimensional carpet was inspired by the parquet floors in the home's entry-way. A low-slung leather armchair designed by Christian Liaigre and a deeply upholstered velvet-clad sofa provide ample seating—the ultimate bedroom luxury.

TROPICAL NOTES

IN THE SHERRY-NETHERLAND

The concept of a residential pied-à-terre (translated from the French for "foot to earth") dates to the early eighteenth century. At the time, it described a temporary lodging for military personnel after they dismounted their horses. Today, the term commonly refers to a home away from home—a second residence typically in a city—used intermittently.

This color-splashed apartment, perched high above the corner of 59th Street and 5th Avenue in the storied Sherry-Netherland, could be considered the quintessential New York City pied-à-terre. Located on the northeast corner of Central Park, it is steps from Bergdorf Goodman and all the boulevard's luxury boutiques. Harry Cipriani, the legendary Venetian eatery, is in the building for when a bellini (fresh peach purée with prosecco) is the order of the day.

My clients, a sophisticated Brazilian couple who spend a few weeks of the year in New York, came to me with a creative brief: They asked me to craft interiors that called to mind the clean-lined silhouettes of Brazilian modernism, inflected with my love of rich saturated colors. In short, they wanted a supremely comfortable home in New York City that alluded to their homeland.

With a subtle reference to the exuberant palette of Rio's Carnival, we settled on lush jewel tones—topaz, tourmaline, amethyst, and aquamarine—set off by deferential shades of crisp white on the moldings and trim. Further advancing the jewelry metaphor, low-slung and clean-lined coffee tables, a glinting ibex-head dining set, and metallic accessories throughout the home add to the excitement.

While equally rich colors are in evidence in the bedroom, we chose a restful, muted neutral for the walls sheathed with Chinese silk that's hand-painted and embroidered with a meandering plum blossom pattern. Roman shades and over-curtains tailored in a coordinating textile soften the interior architecture.

In the entrance gallery, mythologically inspired Greek gazelles leap across a custom carpet that informs the rest of the apartment's color story. Mirroring the walls adds glamour, heightened by the eglomise-mirrored console. The tableau is completed by a vibrant yellow upholstered bench.

PRECEDING OVERLEAF: A custom-designed media cabinet with vibrant, magenta doors divides this graciously scaled room's living and dining areas. A sumptuous, neutral-tone sofa and matching chairs counter the lacquered walls, while a vintage Maison Jansen palm tree floor lamp illuminates the space. A vintage cloisonné parrot perches on the window ledge, quietly extending the lamp's tropical reference. **ABOVE:** Creating a sanctuary for restful slumber is essential for a city pied-à-terre, especially in Manhattan. The walls, window treatments, and carpet envelop the space, creating a cocoon-like feel. A skirted bench at the foot of the bed references the colors in the living area for a seamless transition between rooms. **OPPOSITE:** Abundant sunlight floods the perfectly outfitted marble-tiled bath.
OVERLEAF: A luminous pair of burnished gold mercury glass lamps flank a similarly hued custom button-tufted bed, upholstered in lush silk velvet. The custom embroidered silk wall covering from Fromental adds movement as the branches meander across the walls, answering Diana Vreeland's command for the eye to travel.

DEEPLY PERSONAL

IN THE EAST VILLAGE

I n 2013, we moved our family to London to explore all that life in the UK offers. Reflecting on that time, I remember it as a joyous exploration, especially for my children, Charlie and Isabelle, who reveled in discovering a new culture.

From a professional perspective, English interior design speaks to me, so it was enlightening to be immersed in the aesthetic. There's a focus on ease and comfort. English rooms welcome visitors to come in and relax. If you have ever perused the pages of *The World of Interiors*, you know what I mean. And English designers have an exceptional understanding of color developed in response to the prevailing gray tones of their weather. London will always be an inspiration to a self-proclaimed colorist such as I.

While we were living abroad, I was approached to decorate several projects—both in New York City and in Connecticut—so I had to travel back and forth. Finding a pied-à-terre in New York became necessary to manage the work successfully.

While we had lived in several homes on the Upper East Side, I wanted a new experience. Since I've always been drawn to the East Village, I began looking there. It's one of the last city neighborhoods that retains its pre-globalization authenticity. There's something energetic and youthful about St. Mark's Place, the teaming NYU students on Astor Place, and the vibrant restaurant culture offering everything from lamb tagine at Shukette to pappardelle Bolognese at Il Cantinori.

After seeing nearly fifty apartments in the Village, I settled on one located on an upper floor in a seventeen-story 1920s building—an anomaly in the East Village—with unobstructed, picturesque views of Grace Church, the Empire State Building to the north, and the World Trade Center to the south. It also featured a proper layout with a welcoming entryway, a sun-filled

A vintage Karl Springer tortoise shell serves as the centerpiece of a radiating collection of art and objects in the entryway, including paintings, watercolors, drawings, and tribal masks. Interspersed are works by my daughter, Isabelle. An angular Zig Zag chair by Gerrit Thomas Rietveld, a Parisian flea market mirror, a signed Louis 16th dessert console, and a pair of English Regency chairs energize the tableau. **OVERLEAF:** In the living room, a photograph by Hendrik Kerstens, who recreates old master portraits with his daughter as his subject and muse, stands in dialog with a 1940s painting of the cliffs of Normandy, which was purchased at a flea market in Paris. A deceptively comfortable antique Scottish antler chair, playfully covered in lamb shearling, adds a distinctly sculptural element. The sectional sofa is covered in a Belgian cut velvet of my design.

PRECEDING OVERLEAF: This opposing view of the living room reveals a subtle mélange of textures anchored on an oversized woven jute rug. Other much-loved possessions include a Minotti loveseat covered in lush velvet and an armchair from my childhood. Michael Wolf's photograph of Marina Towers in Chicago establishes a rhythm, complemented by a collection of Picasso-esque rattan bull's head baskets collected in the south of France.
OPPOSITE: Challenging convention, a biomorphic-shaped, gently convexed mirror, which I purchased in Paris, hangs in my apartment's entryway. In the evening, it is awash in the amber glow of an alabaster pendant.
ABOVE: Several pieces of my ever-expanding carved malachite collection perch atop books on one of Christian Astuguevieille's sensational rope-clad tables.

In pondering how to decorate, I thought about my life as a curiosity-filled collector and the many remark- able shopping excursions I have been on.

Each object, artwork, or furnishing in my home represents a story from my life as an interior designer; they reflect my varied interests in, and knowledge of, the decorative arts accumulated on my extensive travels. The unifying threads include my fascination with mixing fine antiques with collectible vintage pieces, a kaleidoscopic celebration of color, and a decidedly maximalist approach to design. Careful curation is also critical; without it, a more-is- more approach invites visual chaos. It takes a trained eye to strike the perfect balance.

living room, and a bedroom with space for seating, all of which appealed to me.

In pondering how to decorate, I thought about my life as a curiosity-filled collector and the many remarkable shopping excursions I have been on. In short, I wanted this home to reflect my life to date, a tangible visual scrapbook brimming with objects and furnishings collected at antique stores throughout the UK and on the weekend excursions we took around Europe—including frequent visits to the Marché aux Puces de Saint-Ouen in Paris. At home in the East Village, I would combine vintage and antique finds from my favorite New York City shops and beyond.

Instead of using my signature saturated colors on the walls, I opted for a palette of warm grays set off by dove white trim so that my collection would become the focus. But there are carefully placed accents too: the entryway ceiling is covered in "Desert Storm," a whimsically colored camouflage motif, and the interior curve of the archway is sheathed in faux bois "London Plane"—both from my wallpaper collection. Moroccan-inspired patterns—a nod to part of my ancestral heritage—appear on the living room sofa and the bedroom's textured rug.

The apartment is a playful mix of myriad styles and eras, with contemporary pieces mixed with classical details. Taken collectively, the rooms tell a deeply personal story of my interests and who I am as a designer. When I open the door at the end of each day, I'm transported to distant locales—and those closer to home—where I collected each of the cherished possessions hanging on the walls, positioned on the floor, or gathered atop a coffee table. In a word, it's my sanctuary.

ABOVE: Hung in the center of this entry wall is a 1943 self-portrait by the 20th-century Italian artist Giacomo Gabbiani, discovered on a shopping trip to Milan. **OPPOSITE:** Emblazoned on the dining room wall is a dynamic mural by the contemporary street artist João Salomão (aka Pixote). The yellow table is a custom design, while the metal-and-leather chairs by Michel Cadestin and Georges Laurent, decommissioned from the Pompidou Center in Paris, provide stylish seating.

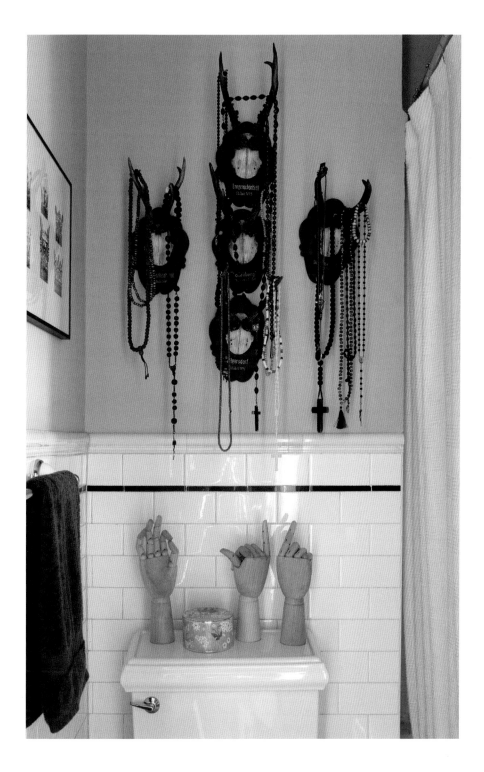

OPPOSITE: A framed series by the Irish abstractionist Ronnie Hughes hangs above a custom button-tufted bed in the bedroom; the bed's diamond motif is repeated on a larger scale in the weave of the Moroccan rug. An iconic Knoll-designed Spoleto chair, one of a pair, adds a color counterpoint with its cherry-red leather. **ABOVE:** While shopping in Copenhagen, I purchased the three carved-wood hands at a Scandinavian design store. I encourage my guests to tuck notes between their fingers. Representing a cross-section of religions, a collection of prayer beads, gathered along my travels, hangs above the commode.

ART DECO-INSPIRED

ON THE UPPER EAST SIDE

On rare occasions, an instant connection occurs in the first client meeting. Such was the case with the vibrant couple who purchased this apartment—the vice chairman of an international beauty brand and his stylish, charismatic wife. From the first handshake, we knew we were meant to work together.

They were living in Asia, and, with their sons off to college, they wanted an empty-nester's pied-à-terre in New York City. They found a gracious two-bedroom apartment within the landmarked limestone-and-brick Barbizon Hotel building on Manhattan's East Side (once the home of Edith Bouvier "Little Edie" Beale). It still had many of its original pre-war details, so we worked to restore and embrace them, retaining a welcome historical gravitas within what would become a glinting jewel box.

In our extensive communications, I discovered my clients share an affinity for the Chinese art deco style, born of the International Exhibition of Modern Decorative and Industrial Arts, held in Paris in 1925. Like many of their counterparts worldwide, Chinese designers and architects adopted French art deco's technological modernity, inherent symmetry, and streamlined geometry—but put their spin on it by including traditional Chinese motifs and patterns. They also employed time-honored Chinese materials like lacquer, indigenous woods, and silks. Many of those motifs and finishes were incorporated into this home's design.

For example, referencing Chinese folklore, wherein mirrors are thought to dispel evil spirits, we clad the apartment's entryway in mirror sheets detailed with a deco-referencing diamond motif at the top and bottom. The ceiling is silver leafed to add to the drama.

On a holistic level, a Chinese-inspired design needs to include red, which culturally symbolizes happiness, success, and good fortune. It's also celebratory, used during special occasions, like festivals and weddings. So, we incorporated red in an octagonal-and-square medallion hand-blocked Gracie wallpaper which I designed specifically for this apartment. Red also appears on the high-gloss lacquered walls, and creative closet door hardware.

Stylized bamboo leaves are embedded in the geometric shapes of this custom-designed Gracie wallpaper. Referencing the 1930s and complementing the living room sofa and chair, brush fringe is sewn into the seams of the side chair and toss pillow. The silver-leafed, winged-heart sconce was sourced through Blackman Cruz in Los Angeles. **OVERLEAF:** High-gloss lacquered walls achieved with nine layers of Hollandlac paint—carefully sanded between coats—add an incomparable depth by reflecting every light source and create a marine-like finish. A diamond-patterned rug references a prevalent motif from the art deco movement. With seating for six, it's a perfect spot to entertain guests in high style.

Complementary shades
of teal and peacock blue
throughout the home
create cohesion—the
yin to red's yang—as you
travel between rooms.

PRECEDING OVERLEAF, LEFT: Set against red lacquer,
a twisting-branch convex mirror designed by the
French master Hervé van der Straeten provides an
intimate reflection of the living room. **PRECEDING
OVERLEAF, RIGHT:** I designed the dining room table
to pay homage to the mirror above. Its glass top
affords an unobstructed view of the naturalist base.
A suite of elegant dining chairs is covered in rich
teal velvet. The vintage ceiling fixture, found at
Bernd Goeckler, bathes the space with an amber
glow. **THIS SPREAD:** The late decorator Mario Buatta
famously said that color should be an expression of
happiness. I wholeheartedly agree. With a grouping
of contemporary ceramics in red, blue, and green;
a collection of mid-century Italian glass vases; red
silk tassels on a closet door; or two dozen blowsy
ranunculus haphazardly arrange on a hall table,
color delights the eye and invigorates daily life. And
saturated colors enliven more so than their softer
counterparts; potent color is dynamic.

In the kitchen, which is relatively small and open to the rest of the home, we opted for a colorful impact by carrying the teal paint across the ceiling.

Complementary shades of teal and peacock blue throughout the home create cohesion—the yin to red's yang—as you travel between rooms.

In Chinese mythology, five tigers keep cosmic forces in balance, preventing chaos from overtaking life. We included a tiger pattern on a deep-cushioned club chair in the living room and a custom banquette in the dining area. A sectional sofa hugs the wall to extend the floor space. Gracie's show-stopping faux tortoiseshell wallpaper was inset between the ceiling beams and then lacquered.

There are American art deco references in the home as well. In a nod to the 1930s decorator Syrie Maugham—one of my design idols heavily influenced by the deco movement—I specified brush fringe be inserted into the seams of a Hollywood Regency-inspired sectional sofa. Animating the tableau, a collection of Lillian Bassman's iconic black-and-white fashion photographs, which I helped my clients acquire, hangs above in salon style.

In the kitchen, which is relatively small and open to the rest of the home, we opted for a colorful impact by carrying the teal paint across the ceiling. Matching mosaic wall tile adds depth, while custom mahogany cabinetry affords storage space to keep appliances hidden.

We found an exciting leopard print carpet for the primary bedroom, originally designed by Madeleine Castaing, who also worked in the 1930s and was influenced by the art deco movement. It inspired the rest of our choices, including an upholstered bed I designed and the rare bronze-mirrored cabinet we found at Donzella in Tribeca.

We adopted a counterintuitive approach in the diminutive galley kitchen, which is open to the apartment's hallway. While the marble floor tile is creamy neutral, the other surfaces are a mix of polished mahogany, teal mosaic tile, and a coordinating high-gloss ceiling. The Roman shades are tailored from one of my textile designs, and they soften the rigid lines of the interior architecture. A pair of sinuous barstools are perfect for enjoying a morning cappuccino. **OVERLEAF:** A custom-colored grass cloth sheaths the primary bedroom walls, providing the perfect backdrop for a cognac-hued, biscuit-tufted velvet bed and a cloverleaf mirror designed by Jean-Bérenger de Nattes. The reflective mica wallpaper on the ceiling extends the ambient light during the day and bathes the room in metallic shimmer by evening lamplight. Hand-carved Moroccan mosharabi panels, a signature detail in my projects, are inset into the window, and the lined-and-interlined silk curtains allow a darkened respite at the end of a kinetic New York City day.

COLOR MEETS PATTERN

IN A TORONTO TOWNHOUSE

S ome say there are two seasons in Toronto: winter and July. Others acknowledge the four seasons as almost winter, winter, still winter, and get-the-beach-towels. If you've spent time in Toronto, you understand. For half the year, shades of gray and white are ubiquitous; there are weeks when evergreen trees seem to provide the only contrast.

As such, you could be forgiven for thinking that Toronto's decorating pendulum would swing toward embracing a broader color spectrum—but as a rule, neutral shades prevail.

The couple—a former screenwriter and a newspaper editor—who purchased this circa 1880s Victorian home were ready to challenge the city's decorative status quo. And so, after seeing my work in a shelter publication and learning of my penchant for vibrant hues, they reached out to have me decorate their light-filled rooms.

The project's first phase involved my clients hiring a Toronto architect to rethink the space. Special attention was paid to retaining the home's character, and the original paneling, archways, and hardwood floors were kept in place. But the home's staircase was repositioned, a powder room was moved, and an expansive primary bath was added on the second floor. After the dust cleared, they had a revitalized floor plan for a family of four.

During our initial discussions about decorating, my clients asked for rooms with bold colors and patterns that reflected their personalities—spaces that would inspire emotional responses and spark joy. Being avid entertainers, they wanted their visitors and guests to know from the first approach that surprises lay within. The front door's exterior was painted a lush Kelly green to set that tone. Then our attention turned to the rooms beyond.

One significant advantage of older Victorians is that they have high ceilings, which allow for bold strokes of color and pattern without shrinking volume. Capitalizing on the opportunity in the living room, I chose the "Vase," a vibrant yellow wallpaper originally designed by David Hicks.

Adjacent to the home's entry vestibule, a tall wood-framed doorway with a charming Victorian pediment leads guests into the expansive living room. The walls beyond are swathed in a cheerful lemon-yellow wallpaper emblazoned with an overscaled chinoiserie pattern that provides a welcome counterpoint in the drab months of Toronto's winter calendar.

One significant advantage of older Victorians is that they have high ceilings, which allow for bold strokes of color and pattern without shrinking volume.

I paired the paper with voluminous silk taffeta curtains, referencing my clients' fashion-forward wardrobe. An overscaled, patterned rug invigorates the floor plane, completing the space.

Furnishings require careful attention in older houses, especially Victorians. You want things to feel in sync with the architectural vernacular, but slavish devotion to period decor can leave you feeling like you're in a museum. We were looking for pieces that referenced the home's history, but that felt contemporary. To fit that brief, I specified classic silhouettes for the upholstery but covered them in fresh colors—cobalt, tangerine, and robin's-egg blue—that modernized the shapes. It's a decorating sleight-of-hand initially favored by the late Dorothy Draper, which remains potent today. And to create a pleasing tension, I chose mid-century pieces—like an iconic 1960s Bubble chair by Eero Aarnio to hang near the bar, and in the study, a cantilevering Lucite Z chair that exudes breezy modernity.

In the dining room, I suggested orange lacquered walls, which a local automotive shop painted on site, and a patterned ceiling. The space is set ablaze in the evening by a dramatic Venetian chandelier. It's a triumphant combination that encourages the lively conversation my clients enjoy, with pieces from their contemporary art collection positioned throughout, sparking interest.

Memories of my clients' childhood vacations in the Bahamas informed the primary bedroom's decor, with walls sheathed in lush, spring-green grass cloth so the couple wakes up to a verdant tropical garden no matter the time of year. A grand-scaled Rhulmann-inspired headboard is balanced by pale hibiscus-pink carpeting.

A monumentally scaled Massimo Vitali beach scene photograph holds court above this corner of the main floor's salon, with deep-seated upholstered pieces positioned to encourage conversation. Refreshing shades of vibrant yellow and blue are tempered with soft mauve gray. A skirted cloverleaf ottoman provides extra seating for entertaining when a larger group is on hand.

Seen one president, seen them all.

Furnishings require careful attention in older houses, especially Victorians. You want things to feel in sync with the architectural vernacular, but slavish devotion to period decor can leave you feeling like you're in a museum.

PRECEDING OVERLEAF LEFT: At one end of the living room, French pocket doors frame the entry to a vibrant tangerine-lacquered dining room, where friends and family regularly gather for meals. Curtains at the far end soften the room's interior architecture. **PRECEDING OVERLEAF RIGHT:** I designed a demilune bar so that everything is at guests' fingertips when it's time for a cocktail hour martini. A high-style vintage chandelier and walls upholstered in channeled velvet infuse the space with 1970s flair. **THIS SPREAD:** This gallery of vignettes underscores my clients' penchant for fearlessly utilizing bright colors and graphic patterns. To cohesively unify and smooth the transitions from room to room, we chose dove white paint for most ceilings, moldings, and walls. Nuanced textures—lush velvet, natural linen, the weave of custom carpets—add tactile sophistication.

OPPOSITE: A suite of drawings by contemporary Dutch artist and draftsman Marcel van Eeden hang in regimental attention in the second-floor study, which doubles as an office. The curtains were fashioned from Josef Frank's iconic "Green Birds" printed linen, which informed the room's color palette. Knoll's Platner coffee table rests on a custom, lattice-patterned rug. **ABOVE:** The interior of the home's curved turret is perfect for relaxing with a beverage from a well-stocked wet bar.

ABOVE: An Empire-style mahogany commode nods to the home's history in the hallway leading to the primary bedroom, where the walls are upholstered in a green-and-white ikat fabric. **RIGHT:** The same ikat pattern covers an art deco-inspired headboard and bed frame. Contemporary bedside tables contrast with a pair of Hollywood Regency-style gilded benches, perfect for changing from shoes to slippers as the day ends.

HISTORICAL REFERENCE

New York City's Lenox Hill neighborhood spans the distance from 68th and 74th streets east of 5th Avenue and was named for Robert Lenox, a Scottish merchant who purchased the then-farmland in 1818. Upon his death in 1939, Lenox's son James inherited the land, which he sold in parcels to be organized into the residential blocks we know today. Some of the finest New York families built homes there, living in Gilded Age extravagance. It remains one of the city's most desirable locales.

On one of the area's finest blocks, this expansive duplex residence occupies the upper floors of a limestone townhouse just a few doors from the fabled building where screen goddess Audrey Hepburn was filmed singing "Moon River" in *Breakfast at Tiffany's*. A young family of four was living on Sutton Place and needed more space, so when this property came on the market, they seized the opportunity and planned their move.

The couple wanted to create rooms that spoke to the history of the townhouse and its neighborhood, focusing on what I consider to be the apogee of American interior design: the 1930s through the 1970s. As avid furniture collectors and New York history buffs, they were well versed in the work of the era's style icons—Dorothy Draper, Billy Baldwin, David Hicks, Albert Hadley, and Sister Parish—each of whom decorated many Lenox Hill homes. So, we researched and referenced those designers' rooms as inspiration for the decorative choices.

When clients approach me with a collection of furniture and decorative elements—especially those of notable provenance—I work to incorporate their existing collections into new rooms while assisting in the acquisition of new pieces, which I find particularly exciting. In this apartment, our goal was to curate an amalgamation of periods and styles, which is the essence of American

An early sconce, one of a pair designed by the legendary twentieth-century French master Lucien Rollin, illuminates this vignette to one side of the apartment's original fireplace. The Georgian demilune table serves as the base for an ever-changing arrangement of cherished belongings, including a painting in the style of Franz Kline and a nineteenth-century Chinese vase from the Qing Dynasty. A delicate arrangement of flowers softens the tableau.

Anchored by a diagonally patterned Stark rug—designed by the incomparable Billy Baldwin—this living room is an artful repository for many pedigreed pieces, including a Jean Royère–style coffee table, klismos chairs and side tables by Robsjohn-Gibbings, a Saarinen side table, and Karl Springer lamps. The eighteenth-century American secretary and a pair of Gustavian carved chairs from the same period lend historical gravitas.

In this apartment, our goal was to curate an amalgamation of periods and styles, which is the essence of American interiors.

Electrifying Tiffany blue and citron yellow pillows with subtle dressmaker details complement the luster-finished brown walls, drawing the eye around this sun-splashed living room. The curtains were tailored from a lush, custom-printed satin emblazoned with the same motifs as on the Duchess of Windsor's Paris apartment curtains. Dove white paint accentuates the eleven-foot ceilings.

A constellation of rare Greek prints purchased at auction from the collection of Sir William Hamilton, the eighteenth-century British envoy extraordinary to Naples, encircles a faux-tortoise mirror of my design. A matching mirror hanging above the fireplace can be seen in the reflection from across the room. The tufted cushion tête-à-tête has a keyhole back, which affords an uninterrupted sight line across the space.

David Hicks
on bathrooms

In the dining room, a large-scale photograph of poppies takes center stage, with the vibrant orange flowers and background referencing the 1970s.

"Java Grande," an iconic wallpaper designed by Jay Spectre for China Seas, animates the dining room walls with kinetic, stylized calligraphy. Two custom armless banquettes flanking the fireplace provide predinner seating. The pewter chandelier once hung in the dining room of the legendary aesthete Harry Hinson's mother's home. A suite of dining chairs in the style of Louis XVI is clad in glove leather and delicate botanical embroidery.

interiors. The rooms mirror our society as an exciting, optimistic melting pot of people from across the globe. American design sparks excitement by perfecting a cross-cultural mix exponentially more significant than its parts.

For me, dark walls recede into the background and place the focus on the furnishings, which move to the visual foreground. In this apartment, I turned to a saturated shade that Billy Baldwin referred to as Coca-Cola brown. (Coincidentally, it is the color he lacquered his oft-photographed studio apartment on East 61st Street, less than ten blocks away.)

In the dining room, a large-scale photograph of poppies takes center stage, with the vibrant orange flowers and background referencing the 1970s when warmer colors—specifically earth tones—reached a zenith in home decor popularity.

Throughout the private spaces on the upper floor are equally notable furnishings, but the color palette is decidedly muted, striking a balance with the communal rooms below. For the bedrooms, memories of stylish beds, down comforters and pillows, sumptuous textiles, and plush upholstery from favorite hotel rooms around the globe were incorporated. It's a decorating strategy I return to repeatedly because, in my view, one of the ultimate luxuries is waking up from a restful night's sleep.

OPPOSITE: A bud vase with three lady slipper orchids, a curvaceous Murano glass lamp, cherished books, and seashells rest atop a Gio Ponti table in this vignette. **ABOVE**: Muted, mint-green grass cloth wraps the perimeter of the primary bedroom, which retains the apartment's original fireplace mantel. The rush basket adds a welcome naturalistic note.

Throughout the private spaces on the upper floor are equally notable furnishings, but the color palette is decidedly muted, striking a balance with the communal rooms below.

RIGHT: A sophisticated pairing of continental silhouettes—an eighteenth-century *fauteuil à la reine* covered in silk and a carved stool of the same period wrapped in velvet—mix with more contemporary pieces in this seating area, including an applied cork mirror in the style of Jean-Michel Frank and a one-armed Jean Pascaud sofa. Together the furnishings underscore the room's Francophile sensibility. **OVERLEAF LEFT:** Two nineteenth-century French drawings hang above a Saarinen table in the daughter's room. The pleated coronet and hanging panels fall into a pale pink tufted headboard, and an overscaled houndstooth check establishes a counterpoint. **OVERLEAF RIGHT:** Four seventeenth-century engravings hang within a 1940s French-style Jean-Charles Moreau curtain treatment in the son's room. The antique walnut Swedish bed was fitted with a Charles Beckley horsehair mattress.

REVISITING GLAMOUR

ON PARK AVENUE

Trusting someone with the intimate task of decorating your home requires a certain camaraderie, an appreciation for their aesthetic vision, and trust in their business acumen. So, the best compliment an interior designer can receive is when a cherished client reaches out to work with you again. That was the case with the recent refresh of this apartment, which I first decorated nearly twenty years ago for a woman with whom I've developed a lasting friendship.

A vibrant, lifelong New Yorker, she grew up a dozen blocks south on Park Avenue in a spacious duplex apartment decorated by her late mother, whose affinity for 1970s decor left my client with an appreciation for that era's unique design zeitgeist. It was a time when projects designed by Angelo Donghia, Jay Spectre, John Saladino, and others were splashed across the highly influential pages of legendary editor Paige Rense's *Architectural Digest*.

With her having such happy memories of her childhood abode, we initially set out to decorate this apartment with similar '70s design references, while softening the high-octane Studio 54 vibe to make the space suitable for her family. But with a change in relationship status and her three children now grown and off on their own, the time had come to reinvent the apartment to express her unique personal style. My directive was clear: more color, more pattern, and an elevated joie de vivre.

One of our first conversations revolved around a shared love for purple—in all its myriad shades. You see it first just inside the apartment where we electrified the demure off-white moldings by painting them the perfect high-gloss lilac. To amplify the drama, the ceiling was papered with one of my favorite geometric designs, "Hicks' Hexagon" by the late David Hicks. A pedestalled statue of Venus and a crystal chandelier, inherited from her mother, inflect the entry gallery with welcome nostalgia.

OPPOSITE: White marble detailed with a stylized cut-key border defines the boundaries of the oversized entryway, which is clad with mirror to reflect ambient light. In the style of Pierre Cardin, the black lacquer cabinet acts as a sideboard when the room is used for large dinner parties. A pair of blue glass lamps illuminate the pen-and-ink drawing by the artist David Paul Kay. **OVERLEAF:** Sophisticated geometric patterns establish a visual dialog in the living room, where a custom oval rug softens the parquet floor. An important stone coffee table by 1970s design legend Karl Springer is surrounded by generous neutral-toned seating. Hanging above a Saint Thomas-style sofa is a work by the celebrated neo-Expressionist Hunt Slonem. The canvas shifts from silver to gold, depending on your vantage point.

Smoothing the transition from the entryway to the adjoining space, we painted both sides of the door in the same lilac hue. It creates a certain frisson juxtaposed against the coral-pink hand-painted wallpaper in the living room, with a pair of Robsjohn-Gibbings chairs covered in tobacco cut velvet balancing the exuberant palette. Just beyond, through a pair of French doors, the adjacent family room was reimagined as a dining room and seating area. Here we took our inspiration from a decorative throw pillow I'd purchased for the apartment, which was covered with an embroidered chrysanthemum motif. I commissioned an artist to recreate the floral pattern, enlarged and custom colored in shades of pink and gold. Shot through with metallic flourish, the wall finishes in both rooms change as the day shifts from dawn to dusk.

We also set about a major kitchen renovation, including significant structural changes. This included paring back an ancillary bathroom to enlarge the space for a generous cooking island. At the far end of the room, a carefully considered laundry area and a breakfast nook for a morning cappuccino were added as part of the new floor plan. For one final 1970s design reference, the sleek custom cabinetry and newly positioned walls were finished in glossy white, calling to mind the late designer Michael Taylor's airy California rooms.

ABOVE: A pair of Murano glass sconces purchased in New York cast an amber glow in the powder room, which is sheathed in a purple-and-white wallpaper of my design. **OPPOSITE:** In one corner of the living room an unusual yellow faux-tortoise desk, once owned by my client's mother, provides desk space. The stylish tableau is completed with a fluted-glass-and-brass mirror, a Fornasetti lamp, and an iconic fiberglass Verner Panton "S" chair. **OVERLEAF LEFT:** A forced-perspective photograph by Doug Hall adds subliminal depth to the seating area in the dining room. The sofa below is upholstered in an iridescent weave, which mixes perfectly with the room's metallic notes. **OVERLEAF RIGHT:** Vintage Ico Parisi dining chairs covered in cream leather surround an Italian glass-and-pedestal dining table. A Gio Ponti mirror hangs above a brass-inlaid sideboard, which doubles as a bar cart.

OPPOSITE: Bold graphic patterns set the tone in the breakfast nook, with a pair of reverse-painted mirrors hanging adjacent to a biomorphic work purchased at an emerging art fair. The chairs are Danish modern which we covered in geometric silk weave. **ABOVE:** An unsightly riser in the middle of the room presented an unusual challenge in the kitchen, so we surrounded it with frosted Lucite, lit from within, reminiscent of Donald Judd's work.

PARISIAN INFLUENCE

IN CARNEGIE HILL

A morning spent in awe of the Nike of Samothrace in the Daru wing of the Louvre, an afternoon of fashionable people-watching in the manicured Tuileries Garden, an evening dining on classic French fare at Le Voltaire on the Seine's left bank: These are a few of my favorite things to do in Paris. But as anyone who has visited the City of Lights can attest, there is infinitely more to do and see. Frequent visitors know a universal truth about Paris: It is impossible to get bored there. The city reveals itself to the adventurer over time with each meandering visit.

The couple that owns this apartment are world travelers, so our work together began with lengthy conversations about their many trips abroad and, for the gentleman of the house, his frequent trips to Paris for work. Pondering their travels, they expressed the wish to have a New York City home reflective of the breezy, unhurried European lifestyle they have come to appreciate. Light-filled rooms with quality pieces arranged in a casual style became the brief.

But long before any decorative decisions could be made, structural work needed to be done, as this home began as two apartments that we combined. To accomplish that task, we worked with a talented French architect well versed in the ways the French detail space.

Setting the pace, we worked together to create an octagonal vestibule just inside the apartment's front door, inspired by a room I discovered in a rare copy of the 1930s French periodical *Maison de France*, which documented the work of the renowned architect-designers of the time—Jean-Charles Moreux, Jansen, and Le Corbusier, among others.

Turning our focus to the home's furnishings, myriad cultures and periods were mixed. Still, we were principally influenced by the Directoire style, born in the latter half of the eighteenth century, immediately following the French Revolution. In this period, while often imbued with

High-gloss black lacquered walls wrap the perimeter of the apartment's octagonal entryway. The color and finish reference the Parisian entry hall and dining room of Jansen's director Pierre Delbee, trimmed in the same creamy shade as seen here. A Directoire-style chest, an American carved chair, and an Austrian crystal chandelier add cross-cultural notes.

Like many Parisian apartments, the living room is enveloped in crisp white paint, which amplifies the sunlight as it bounces around the space. As the couple are bibliophiles, books feature prominently on their custom built-in shelves, punctuated by a pair of small French art deco sconces purchased in New York. The red glass lamps are Chinese, but here reference the façade of the Moulin Rouge on the Boulevard de Clichy in Paris's 18th arrondissement.

neoclassical motifs, furniture silhouettes were pared back, evidencing a certain simplicity and rejecting many of the predominant themes associated with royal extravagance. That conceptual restraint was an overarching theme, notably seen in the custom millwork throughout this apartment: The pediment and pilasters in the living room bookcases, for example, where rare and out-of-print volumes reveal the interests and idiosyncrasies of the homeowners.

The couple had a collection of old-master drawings in gilt frames from the seventeenth, eighteenth, and nineteenth centuries and asked that they be highlighted in the apartment's muted, tone-on-tone dining room. My thoughts turned to the prestigious Paris Salon, which began in 1673 and continues to this day, when people from across Europe and beyond travel to see works of art in dizzying displays. (It is where the concept of hanging art salon style began, with painting and drawings hung in proximity to each other.)

To contrast the neutral shades in the dining room, I chose a lavish, saturated color palette for the family room, where the walls are upholstered in an espresso brown cashmere-and-wool stripe, and the floor is covered with a rich crimson carpet. The space conjures visions of an elegant Parisian hotel lobby, which reminds the homeowners it's time to book their next trip to France.

ABOVE: In the kitchen, a custom-designed table built by York Street Studio is flanked by a vibrant red banquette and a similarly hued Knoll-designed Spoleto chair. **OPPOSITE:** A custom corner banquette upholstered in one of my fabrics invites casual conversation in this study. An exceptional faux-tortoise mirror purchased through Gregorius Pineo glows in the light of a pair of diminutive, mirrored ceiling fixtures.

An array of gilt-framed old-master drawings animates the walls of this dining room nook, outfitted with a pair of square tables in the style of Jean-Michel Frank, which can be joined together for larger gatherings. The cabana-striped banquette visually tames the artwork's riotous arrangement, while an André Arbus-inspired rug with a singular woven border grounds the space.

Pondering their travels, they expressed the wish to have a New York City home reflective of the breezy, unhurried European lifestyle they have come to appreciate.

In the primary bedroom, neutral-toned grass cloth-covered walls encourage peaceful sleep; above, a faux bois wallpaper covers the space between the ceiling beams, adding a naturalistic motif. Feminine touches—a collection of delicate blue vases and a pair of lithe French lamps—play against a button-tufted wool-satin headboard and a 19th-century Baltimore dresser with its original hardware. The striped acrylic sculpture is by Michael Laube.

OPPOSITE: In the hallway en route to the bedrooms, two Calyxte Campe portraits immortalize the family's children. A 19th-century Swedish alabaster ceiling fixture purchased in Paris and an 18th-century console desserte complete the tableaux. ABOVE: A luminous undersea photograph by Renato Freitas informs the color palette in the son's room with walls sheathed in cool-toned grass cloth.

IN THE COUNTRY

A 19TH-CENTURY RETREAT

IN LITCHFIELD COUNTY

While rooms tell stories about their inhabitants, on a more macro level, houses tell stories, too, about how and where they are in the world. And to follow that logic, the best homes, and their decoration, should feel at one with their geography and—at least in some ways—in keeping with the history and tradition of a place. To put a finer point on it, you wouldn't decorate a Palm Beach penthouse in the style of Aspen ski lodge or vice versa. This sense of relativity was my primary concern for designing and decorating this 1840s eyebrow Colonial farmhouse in Washington, Connecticut, which my wife Lisa and I purchased in 2009.

Initially located in the center of town on a quaint road by the bank of the Shepaug River, the house was painstakingly moved to its current location in the 1950s, positioned on a seven-acre parcel of bucolic New England countryside. The rolling topography and expansive setback from the road—unheard of in the era of horse-drawn carriages—were two of the house's best-selling points.

With experience decorating farmhouses, I first meticulously surveyed the house. What remained of the original floor plan? Had the house expanded over its history? Had any of those additions detracted from the house's historical integrity? What materials and finishes should be restored? The answers to these questions—and many more—directly informed the work ahead.

As a well-maintained historic house, there were many appealing details: a generously scaled front porch; the original staircases, doors, and fireplaces; patinated wrought iron hardware; float-glass windows; and beautifully weathered wide-plank floors. The kitchen needed an update, but I paid close attention to the architectural vocabulary of nineteenth-century farmhouses by keeping it simple, retaining rough-hewn beams and open shelving, and sensitively bridging the historical with contemporary functionality.

OPPOSITE: A pair of glass-topped vintage luggage racks serve as coffee tables, perched in front of a vintage bamboo sofa and chair, which were revitalized with a fresh coat of paint. The porch ceiling was finished in glacier blue, a decorating detail popularized in the American South in the early 1800s. The striped outdoor carpet echoes the lines of the picket rail, imposing a regimental sense of order.
OVERLEAF: A pair of marine-blue,19th-century English acid jars atop a farmhouse table add a splash of color to the family room. At left, an early Vermont pie safe from the same period serves as storage space for tableware and linens. The set of spindle-back chairs was purchased with the house and painted matte black. The walls are painted in Benjamin Moore's Willow Creek.

RIGHT: Soft gray and gold veining defines the newly organized kitchen's single-slab Imperial Danby marble countertop. At right, an 18th-century Dutch "kas" cabinet, made in the Hudson River Valley from indigenous gumwood, affords a clutter-free dry bar. A sculptural wooden assemblage by the late artist Richard Faralla hangs in the stairwell, complementing a Hendrik Kerstens work, which combines Dutch masters imagery and contemporary photography. **OVERLEAF, LEFT:** A set of kitchen stools in the style of the Bauhaus movement introduces a modern silhouette in the kitchen, which is flooded with natural light. Other modern elements include a Wolf cooktop and fittings from Waterworks. **OVERLEAF, RIGHT:** A side door is coated in a high-gloss, custom shade of dusty aubergine paint I created for this house. The collection of walking sticks stands ready to be pressed into service for strolls in the surrounding woodland.

Tropical foliage, depicted in classic grisaille fashion, meanders across the hand-painted Gracie wallpaper in the dining room. The furnishings are an eclectic mélange of periods and styles, including a custom dining table in the style of Jean-Michel Frank, a suite of chairs designed by Richard Rogers and Renzo Piano, and an 18th-century pine dry sink from Vermont. A varied collection of amethyst glass, arranged on a deep windowsill, references the glass collection at Beauport.

I paid close attention to the architectural vocabulary of nineteenth-century farmhouses by keeping it simple, retaining rough-hewn beams and open shelving, and sensitively bridging the historical with contemporary functionality.

With the structural changes realized, my work turned to the decoration of the house, and here, I took my inspiration from the interiors of late nineteenth-century and early twentieth-century New England houses, an in particular from the forty-room Sleeper-McCann house in Gloucester, Massachusetts.

Now a National Historic Landmark, Beauport, as the Sleeper-McCann home is affectionately called, was the ground-up creation of Henry Davis Sleeper, who is widely regarded as one of America's first professional interior designers. It is unique among houses in that each room was decorated with a theme in mind, with no two spaces the same. I've had the pleasure of visiting Beauport on several occasions. Some of my favorite rooms in the house are the China Trade room, which features hand-painted Chinese wallpaper and Asian ephemera; the curious Octagon room, painted slate blue with robust orange accents; and its Center Hall, which is luminescent, populated with 150 pieces of amber glass. Sleeper's catholic style appeals to me with furnishings collected from all over the country, and, in the case of Beauport, from all over the world.

In my view, we can trace Sleeper's eclecticism to the country's founding fathers: Thomas Jefferson, for example, whose Monticello has New York shield-back dining chairs next to an Italian marble-topped tea table below an ornate French mirror. Mixing cross-culturally in fresh and exciting ways, drawing inspiration from all corners of the globe, is the essence of American interiors.

On one side of the living room, a 19th-century stool by Wallace Nutting and an 18th-century English demilune console rest at the base of the house's colonial staircase. The original newel post and railing were fashioned from native cherry wood. A mounted amethyst geode glows in the light of a French bouillotte lamp throughout the evening.

In the living room, a custom-made sofa, upholstered in a muted wool plaid fabric of my design, is paired with nailhead-detailed club chairs in the style of Maison Jansen. A 1970s brass-antler coffee table adds a metallic note, perched atop a geometric carpet of my design in shades of red and cream. The spruce-green lamps were made from antique French wine bottles.

Set against neutral wallpaper, plaid textiles, and paint shades, the house is inflected with colorful moments, like a polychrome collection of blue pottery in a hallway, and purple glassware in the dining room. My daughter Isabelle's bedroom, upper right, is enveloped in spring-green grass cloth, mirroring the verdant landscape outside the window. (She personally requested the zebra curtains and bedspread!)

In the primary bedroom, an acrylic sculpture by Michael Laube hangs above an upholstered bed and headboard, clad in a fabric of my design. Flat Roman shades, tailored in a stylized floral design by Albert Hadley, darken the room for restful sleep; the textile is seen repeated on shams and pillows. Contemporary sconces illuminate a 19th-century American nightstand, while a chaise by Jean Pascaud is paired with a bench by Valentin Loellmann.

ABOVE: In the guest bedroom, antique linen-clad twin beds are nestled below an evocative 19th-century photograph of Rome's Colosseum. **OPPOSITE:** Antonio Citterio's Carlotta chair, covered in zebra hide, is juxtaposed against a Duncan Phyfe Empire sofa and a Chinese taboret table. The photograph depicts a deconstructed bird's nest by the contemporary American artist Randy West. **OVERLEAF:** A collection of iconic outdoor furniture designed by Richard Schultz (who joined Knoll in 1951 to work with Harry Bertoia) is arranged around the organic-edged pool in the backyard. Old-growth trees populate the landscape, further developed to include a garden with many indigenous plants.

DESTINATION SPOT

ON A FAMILY COMPOUND

I designed and decorated the main house on this property twenty years ago for a family who, after many happy years there, decided to sell it in favor of a larger dwelling nearby. In a serendipitous twist, the new owners, full-time New York City residents, purchased it as a weekend home in 2017 and contacted me.

They admired the interiors I had created for the previous owners and, as architectural enthusiasts interested in preservation, asked if I would help them turn the century-old, brick-red barn on their acreage into a "destination" spot for gatherings of friends and family—essentially a home-away-from-home on their new property.

Long beyond its original agricultural purpose, the barn, now empty and underutilized, had fallen into a dilapidated condition. Breathing new life into it would require a complete structural restoration, so I engaged East Coast Barn Builders to shepherd the construction project. We aimed to create a building with an instantly recognizable rural silhouette and interiors ideally suited for recreational activities throughout the four seasons.

In our initial meeting, my clients presented a unique problem: Save an old-growth copper beech tree encroaching on the structure. Our solution? We built a new foundation—from local fieldstone—for the barn a few yards closer to the house, then moved the building—beams, siding, rafters, and hardware—to its new location.

To capitalize on the barn's airy volume, my team programmed the building into a grand-scaled room at one end, the ceiling open to the rafters, with a generous seating area and dining room. Additionally, since one of the owners is an avid cook, we created an expansive chef's kitchen adjacent to the large vegetable garden just outside. At the other end of the interior, we organized two loft spaces accessible from dedicated staircases—one as a welcoming guest bedroom and bath and the other as a playroom for the family's three children.

Moved several yards from its original location on the property and nestled into a cropping of indigenous trees, the newly situated barn feels like it has always been there. We worked with a team specializing in barn restoration, so the entire exterior was constructed from the building's original wood, augmented with reclaimed materials where necessary.

ABOVE: Full-length curtains tailored from a stylized floral print introduce an organic motif, softening the interior architecture at the base of a staircase leading to a guest bedroom. **OPPOSITE:** With a state-of-the-art sound system and a retractable screen hidden at the top of the stone hearth, the main living space is easily transformed for movie night. A constellation of glass shades radiates from a monumentally scaled Pouenat chandelier, which casts a glow on the pickled ceiling, accentuating the room's height.

Considering the barn's interior furnishings, we purchased an eclectic mix, seamlessly combining antique, vintage, and custom pieces.

THIS SPREAD: Hand-hewn beams and rafters in the barn's creamy white interior establish a naturalistic connection to the verdant landscape just beyond the barn's many double-hung windows. Rich textures—woven leather, plain-weave linen, polished stone—further allude to the building's relationship with the outdoors. The custom-designed ottoman in front of the fireplace serves as a coffee table and a footrest. OVERLEAF: While the dove-white kitchen is all new, juxtapositional materials and finishes call to mind the nostalgia of a bygone era: subway tiles against oak floors, Imperial Danby marble on the island against honed black granite countertops, open glass cabinets flanking the sink against solid door fronts surrounding the stove and Sub-Zero refrigerator. The contemporary ceiling pendants are from Ann Morris.

OPPOSITE: I designed a custom upholstered headboard and bed frame to fit seamlessly into a crossbeam wall in the lofted guest bedroom. The translucent Roman shades were tailored from the celebrated mid-century Swedish designer Josef Frank's Gröna Fåglar print. **ABOVE:** Antique marble floor tiles and a vintage-style porcelain tub stand in contrast to a contemporary glass shower enclosure in the adjacent guest bathroom. The canvas of calligraphic squares, in the style of Franz Klein, adds a perfect black-and-white note.

A pair of asymmetrical built-in
bookcases, calling to mind the
perpendicular lines of a Piet
Mondrian canvas, were
initially designed to house the
pair of tall ceramic lanterns I
purchased on a shopping trip
to Paris. We recessed a wet
bar on the left and a flat-
screen television on the right
to add functionality. The
Raphael Fenice–designed
infinity mirror above the
fireplace was purchased
through the Portuondo
Gallery. A round mosaic
coffee table, surrounded by
two "Key West" outdoor sofas
from Roberti, rests atop a
blue-on-blue geometric
flat-weave rug.

Considering the barn's interior furnishings, we purchased an eclectic mix, seamlessly combining antique, vintage, and custom pieces. Myriad textures, burnished colors, and classic patterns were melded to enhance the effect. This layering is essential when decorating an older structure as you want to avoid an interior that feels stark or overtly modern.

With the barn project nearing completion, my clients expanded the project scope to include moving a poorly sited swimming pool to a more accessible location. We were also asked to design a three-room pool house and pergola-covered patio. With a center seating area and wet bar open to the pool through custom folding doors, a gym to the left, and a billiards room to the right, the additional building welcomes family and guests in the summer months. Turning my attention to the pool house furnishings, I found eager collaborators in my clients, who, in addition to taking a keen interest in pieces purchased at home, traveled to Paris to meet me for a delightful shopping excursion. We visited some of my favorite antique dealers and meandered the flea markets; the pieces we purchased there are welcome visual reminders of that trip to France.

As a designer, I work to create spaces that my clients want to return to again and again, so when this family decided to make this their full-time residence, I considered our collaboration on the property a success.

ABOVE: In the billiard room, my "Eleuthera" wallpaper, depicting stylized ferns and fronds, climbs the walls from the horizontal beadboard to the ceiling. A six-armed lantern illuminates the space after dark. **OPPOSITE:** In this view of the living area, a tall sculptural chair—another Paris flea market find—mixes with an African chieftain stool and a woven Jacques Adnet armchair. The sophisticated diamond-patterned Moroccan tile below the flat-weave rug adds another dimension to the floor plane. **OVERLEAF:** Outside the pool house, through custom accordion doors, a bluestone patio surrounds a newly constructed gunite pool, ideally suited for warm weather swims. Wisteria climbs up and across a crisp white pergola, painting a swath of purple across the late spring landscape. As the years advance, the cedar shake roof will patina to rich driftwood gray.

GLOBAL NOTES

IN WASHINGTON, CONNECTICUT

I'm often asked what makes a truly successful room. The answer is simple: surround yourself with comfortable furnishings you love and objects that bring you joy. Whether you're a minimalist with a few rigorously chosen pieces or a maximalist with layered elements throughout doesn't matter. In the words of the late Billy Baldwin, "Be faithful to your own taste, because nothing you really like is ever out of style."

The avid decorative art collectors who purchased this 1920s Connecticut colonial understand that idea. Over the years, they have amassed a fantastic array of pieces from around the globe: African masks, Swedish beds, English tables, French chairs, and more. In surveying their collections, it became clear my task in decorating this home would be to fit the myriad pieces together—along with art, objects, and furnishings I would add to the mix—in a way that revealed the stories behind their globally inflected style.

But before the rugs were laid or sofas placed upon them, there were paint colors, wallpaper, and fabrics to be chosen. Using a jigsaw puzzle analogy, you start by putting the edges together and then work toward the pieces in the middle as the image—or room—comes into focus.

With colors and patterns, my clients shared my appreciation for rich saturated hues and demonstrative motifs. To set the tone for the rest of the interiors, we settled on one of my all-time favorite wallpapers, "The Vase," originally designed by David Hicks, in fig brown and crisp white to sheath the entryway. Like a leitmotif in a musical composition, shades of brown appear throughout the house as an underlying theme connecting the rooms, each with its own personality.

In the living room, for example, Farrow & Ball's Tanner Brown covers the walls from the baseboard to the modest-profile crown molding, which we painted in Benjamin Moore's White Dove to heighten the contrast. The room's furnishings take you on a veritable whirlwind tour, with

A pair of distressed Swedish chairs; a 19th-century English faux-bamboo, marble-topped hall table; and a gilt-wood framed mirror animate the entryway welcome guests with a hint of the eclecticism that unfolds throughout the house. The patinated banister and painted spindles are original to the house, while the muted-stripe stair runner, sourced through Woodard & Greenstein, is based on an Early American design. **OVERLEAF:** Unassuming white linen Roman shades soften the late afternoon sun in the living room, where seemingly disparate silhouettes combine to create an exciting tableau. The coffee table and zebra-clad stools, designed by Josef Frank, are from my clients' collection. In the corner, a Georgian vitrine—the repository for my clients' antique teacups—stands next to an antique Biedermeier sofa, which we upholstered in one of my favorite stripes.

Using a jigsaw puzzle analogy, we started by putting the edges together and then worked toward the pieces in the middle as the room came into focus.

stops in Germany with the addition of an antique Biedermeier sofa, pieces from England like an heirloom grandfather clock, and a visit to Sweden, evidenced in a Josef Frank printed sofa. A casually arranged group of artwork, some by the family's children, hangs above, while on another wall, African masks create a dialog with two Thebes stools covered in zebra-print linen.

We extended the Scandinavian reference in the dining room by using shades of white and cream favored by Northern Europeans as the antidote to their locale's short days and bleak weather. For dining, two sets of mismatched milk-painted chairs and a Swedish table nod to one of the homeowner's ancestry, all illuminated by a whimsical antler-inspired chandelier. Dark-stained floorboards ground the space like a pine forest floor.

Upstairs in the home's private quarters, one bedroom is wrapped in a British wallpaper depicting a regimented aspen forest rendered in shades of lavender and white; in another, an Italian wallpaper swirls with gray and white storm clouds brewing across the walls and ceiling. The guest bedroom's walls are papered with a classic French toile de Jouy, with musicians and maidens galavanting in the Provençal countryside.

Dynamic and ever-changing as new pieces are collected and added to the mix, the rooms of this house will grow to reflect new chapters in my clients' lives in the years to come. And as a collector myself, that is a very appealing idea.

PRECEDING OVERLEAF: Dueling botanical prints, one upholstered on the Bridgewater arm sofa and the other fashioned into toss cushions, add to the riotous mix in this living room vignette. To the left, an English gentleman's shaving cabinet serves as an end table; on the opposite side, a pine scalloped-edge pedestal table softens the geometry. A pair of kudu antlers hang above, referencing the African continent. **OPPOSITE:** A dozen pieces of rare, mid-century Swedish pottery from my clients' collection are arranged across the white dove mantel in the living room, which is grounded by an interlocking diamond-patterned sisal rug. Warm, earthy tones from sandstone to lush espresso connect the rooms, leading the eye's discovery from one space to the next. A densely populated hat rack adds personality to the entryway. **OVERLEAF:** In the home's tone-on-tone dining room, a Gustavian mirror hangs on "Chiavi Segrete," a Milanese wallpaper designed by Piero Fornasetti. Look closely and see golden keys hanging from the delicately rendered foliage. Blue-and-white porcelains—some Chinese, some English transferware—introduce a whisper of color. For dinner parties, antique Swedish candle sconces cast a romantic glow.

The celebrated interior decorator Bunny Williams once wrote, "What is always important to remember is that rooms are for living, not just for show." It's a sentiment that guides me in my work. Here, organized around a Mies van der Rohe Barcelona table, down-wrapped cushions on deep-seated sofas and chairs welcome family and friends to sit back and relax. The bookshelves are lined with patterned bookbinding paper, adding another layer to the room.

OPPOSITE: An 18th-century English regency scroll-arm desk chair, outlined with care-worn gilding, is paired with a French refractory table in this corner of the light-filled family room. **ABOVE:** On one side of the breakfast room, a carved Scandinavian daybed is upholstered in crisp creme-toned canvas. The floor, covered in a classic-cut French limestone pattern, echoes the color palette. Flirty slipcovers soften the dining chairs.

PRECEDING OVERLEAF, LEFT: With the addition of a running-wall shelf that I designed, the once-awkward hallway leading to the primary bedroom suite has become a destination for contemplating an ever-expanding collection of black-and-white photography. **PRECEDING OVERLEAF RIGHT:** In the primary bedroom, a carved Swedish bed is covered in Italian linens. Antique Chinese bedside tables and a ticking-striped French chair—one of a pair—add international flair. **ABOVE:** Cole & Son's iconic "Woods" wallpaper in color Parme creates a mystical, fairy-tale backdrop for the furnishings in this children's room, including a pair of 19th-century carved and painted beds. A wooden cabinet (opposite, presumably made in 1865) used as toy storage, and a Danish burled-wood pedestal table. A contemporary stacked-Lucite lamp illuminates in the evening, while Marimekko sheets add painterly whimsy. **OVERLEAF:** A suite of 17th-century European engravings, centered between the windows, was the springboard for the color palette in this high-styled guest bedroom, which is wrapped—walls and ceiling—in Fornasetti's "Nuvolette" wallpaper. The twin beds, cozily covered with Thorsøn Norwegian polar bear blankets, share a centered Biedermeier table.

Shades of raspberry, tempered pink, and charcoal gray combine in the daughter's bedroom. Curiously contrasting silhouettes—an American wing chair covered in boiled wool, Arne Jacobsen's Swan sofa clad in textural bouclé, and an unpretentious pine *secrétaire à abattant*—occupy this corner. The geometric canvas, reminiscent of works by Frank Stella, is from my clients' collection.

Botanical illustrator Albert Stockdale's iconic "Martinique" wallpaper conjures a banana plantation fantasy in the pool house, calling to mind the Beverly Hills Hotel where the pattern was first used. Tiger-patterned indoor/outdoor fabric cushions and a suite of woven seagrass furniture underscore the tropical theme. Teak doors close the room off from the elements.

1750s COLONIAL

IN PICTURESQUE NEW ENGLAND

In 1734, one Joseph Hurlbut organized the eastern section of what is now Washington, Connecticut, marking the beginning of the town's settlement by colonists. And while the identity of the original owners of this 1750s center-hall Colonial—considered one of the oldest houses in the area—is unknown, it is reasonable to conclude that they were acquainted with Mr. Hurlbut, his family, and the other early inhabitants of Litchfield County.

I had driven past the house—located a stone's throw from my Connecticut property— countless times over the years, often stopping to admire its symmetry and scale. Unassuming yet perfectly refined, it struck me as the perfect early New England house. So it was quite a compliment to be asked to reinvigorate the structure when a couple I have worked with on another home (just across the street) purchased it as a guesthouse for their property.

As I carefully considered the rooms, it became clear that telling the story of this 270-year- old house would have two distinct chapters: The first about respecting the eighteenth-century architectural heritage and the second about creating a twenty-first-century respite for my clients' sojourning friends and family.

Since the house had fallen into a neglected state, the best course of action was to strip it back to its internal timbers, cataloging and preserving what we could. For example, the mantels were saved; the fireplace and chimney were carefully reconstructed from the original bricks; the wide- plank floors were refurbished with respect for their time-honored patina; and wrought iron hardware was lovingly removed to be reinstalled when the construction phase was complete.

Taking the internal structure back to the studs also allowed us to install new wiring and plumbing, bringing the building up to current codes. And speaking of codes: the narrow and perilously steep front staircase would have needed to be replaced—an unpalatable proposition when you're trying to maintain a structure's historical sensibility—so we added a second staircase near the back of the house, satisfying local regulations. We also installed insulation

With indigenous-wood clapboards replacing the rotted siding and a fresh coat of crisp white paint, the exterior was returned to its former glory. The original door remains, now painted in Benjamin Moore's Willow Creek. A pair of contemporary sconces in the style of early American fixtures are by Ann Morris. We added globe boxwoods to soften the structure's geometry.

A collection of antique, annotated French botanical drawings in the living room hangs above the original Roxbury granite hearth. Additional drawings are hanging at the bottom of the stairs. A striped runner, woven in a historical pattern, climbs the treads to the second floor. The silver-plate hurricane lamps on the right were purchased from a New York dealer.

and a modern HVAC system for indoor comfort throughout the four seasons.

The original floor plan called for three bedrooms and a full bath on the second floor, providing generous sleeping space for guests, but not quite enough to accommodate extended family. With that in mind, my clients expressed a wish for another bedroom, which presented a significant challenge: local zoning laws dictate that historical houses in Washington maintain their original footprint. My solution was to replace an underutilized shed at the back of the house with a new structure housing a primary bedroom and adjoining bath.

With the spaces organized and wallboards in place, it was time to add the interior millwork, and here I took my cues from the research I had done on other historic houses in the area, adopting a prevalent less-is-more approach. The windows and doors are trimmed with modest profiles. In some rooms, I specified simple chair rails; in others, I added wainscotting or beadboard ceilings. To avoid a sense of rigid accuracy, we took liberties in the new primary bedroom by installing a boarded tray ceiling and built-in cabinetry based on a Scandinavian design as an homage to my clients' ancestry.

OPPOSITE: The dining room fireplace, also original to the house, adds ambiance for cool fall and winter dinners. A custom table, fashioned in the style of a Georgian tripod example, is paired with a collection of upholstered Swedish chairs. Josef Frank's iconic stylized "Window" print was tailored into unlined Roman shades, extending the Scandinavian reference. ABOVE: A contemporary electrified tole tin sconce, one of a pair, casts a soft evening glow. OVERLEAF LEFT: A contemporary bobbin chair, covered in a houndstooth check of my design, is casually paired with an armless sofa in the library. A Saarinen table atop a cowhide rug provides a spot for books and refreshments. The bookshelves are painted in Tanner Brown from Farrow & Ball. The Roman shades are in ticking stripes—also of my design. OVERLEAF RIGHT: An antique English bench and a 19th-century umbrella stand mix in the austere entryway. The front door's cast-iron bell is one of the house's original details.

PRECEDING OVERLEAF: A deep-cushioned sectional sofa, covered in vintage mattress ticking, and two 1940s French leather club chairs, afford abundant seating for eight in this living room. Windowpane-checked Roman shades and patterned pillows—some fashioned from fabrics collected on my clients' trips abroad—add splashes of red to the mix. A coarse-woven jute rug introduces texture underfoot.
RIGHT: Classic Swedish design details meld to create a breakfast room that speaks to my clients' family heritage: painted X-back chairs slipcovered with demure skirts, a crisp-lined antique trestle table, and a Gustavian sideboard embellished with a lyre motif. Below the chair rail, horizontal wallboards are juxtaposed against the wide-plank oak floors, which are left bare, showcasing their rich patina.

PRECEDING OVERLEAF: In the kitchen, vintage farmhouse cabinets, salvaged from one of my clients' previous residences, are detailed with simple wrought iron hardware. The maple butcher block-topped island and honed granite counters provide plenty of work surface when preparing meals. We introduced Moroccan tile as the backsplash between the Viking stove and exhaust hood. The pair of Urban Electric pendants add a modern note. RIGHT: An important Swedish flat-weave rug, rendered in shades of cream, mint green, and red accents, anchors a seating area on the second-floor landing. The suite of mid-century Swedish furniture wears its original upholstery in two colors of lush, nubby bouclé, and is accessorized with a shearling hide. The antique painted cabinet just adjacent to the stairs is a family heirloom.

OPPOSITE: A stylish spindle bed, which I had painted a custom color, adds a sculptural element to this guest bedroom. The French bergère chair, brought to this house from another of my clients' residences, is covered in a classic blue and yellow toile de Jouy. An American striped carpet underfoot and a festooned and painted mirror complete the tableaux. **ABOVE:** A barn-red antique side chair adds visual interest at the top of the stairs.

ABOVE: A thoroughly exuberant floral pattern by mid-century master Josef Frank wraps the walls and ceiling of the first floor's new primary bath, which features a deep porcelain tub. I added the repurposed 1920s bay window to flood the room with light. **OPPOSITE:** A daybed built into a Gustavian cabinet, an unusual wingback chair, and an English settee provide bountiful seating in the primary bedroom. Repeating squares—the boarded tray ceiling and crisp-lined four-poster bed—mimic the floor plan.

Two beautifully detailed, 19th-century carved Gustavian beds dressed in stripes, tartan, and a camouflage textile (of my design for Baker furniture) are separated by a vibrant blue painted bench in this guest bedroom. The window treatments were tailored in a Provençal-inspired floral pattern by Kathryn M. Ireland.

SEASIDE RESIDENCE

IN WATCH HILL, RHODE ISLAND

Originally opened as a luxurious seaside hotel in 1868, Ocean House, in Watch Hill, Rhode Island, catered to affluent summer travelers for nearly 150 years until, having fallen out of popularity, it closed its doors to visitors in 2003. The original, sprawling structure sat empty for several years before developers demolished it in 2005 to clear the land for five private homes. But local residents banded together to scuttle that plan.

Fortuitously, an investor stepped in to purchase the property with a proposal to build a new hotel, nearly mirroring the original Victorian structure right down to the butter-yellow façade, cedar shake roof, and sprawling terraces. The plan met with rousing approval, and the new-yet-old Ocean House, with forty-nine rooms and suites and twenty-one private residences, opened to guests in the summer of 2010. Shortly after, I was approached to design and decorate one of the largest corner apartments.

Exceptional within the Ocean House structure, this home features a living room with a working fireplace, two spacious bedrooms, and a sun-drenched private terrace perfect for sunbathing or alfresco meals. But the most exciting room in this home is a turret pavilion with 360-degree views of the ocean and the surrounding land, which, perhaps counterintuitively, I opted to utilize as a large dining room for entertaining family and friends.

In juxtaposition to the exterior's Gothic influences and intricately designed woodwork, I created the interiors to strike a balance, incorporating contemporary furnishings that afford twenty-first-century comfort for the summer residents. And because it faces the sea, I added judiciously chosen nautical details throughout the rooms—without being heavy-handed with oceanside metaphors.

The interior color palette was drawn directly from the landscape, with pale oceanic blues, sea glass green, and spring-bloom lavender; warm neutral tones appear in sand-toned, grass cloth-covered walls in the entryway, matchstick blinds in the windows, and weathered-oak furniture.

Situated at one corner of the home's sizeable teak terrace is a summer-season pavilion I outfitted as a dining room for casual meals. Though the construction is new, the contemporary architect relied on the original plans and included all the charming Victorian details that were part of the hotel's original turret. The exterior columns are repeated inside.

ABOVE: In the glass cloth-lined entryway, two surfboards act as wall sculptures above a trestle bench positioned for easy shoe removal. Just beyond the archway, a series of wave-motif laser-cut metal panels inspired by the Great Wave by the Japanese artist Katsushika Hokusai serve as a room divider. OPPOSITE: The copper-lined fireplace takes the chill off the night air on cooler evenings. Soft, sea glass-inspired colors draw your eye around the cozy living room.

THIS SPREAD: In successful rooms, it's all in the carefully considered details. Here, custom built-in bookshelves lined with book-binding paper in the living room, twin beds dressed in apricot cashmere blankets in the guest bedroom, and an upholstered banquette paired with a zinc-topped trestle table in the breakfast nook all add to the quintessential New England charm. In the primary bedroom, a soft-pink, button-tufted headboard lends a feminine note.

OVERLEAF: I designed the round dining table with an architectural, bleached-wood base, which is set back to provide guests with ample leg room. The top is upholstered in lavender wool felt that we trimmed with antique bronze nail heads; it muffles the sounds so guests can enjoy the rhythm of ambient rolling waves. The woven-seat dining chairs are Danish, while above, a humble fisherman's net was fashioned into a pendant fixture outfitted with a single Edison bulb.

ACKNOWLEDGMENTS

First, I would like to thank Carl Dellatore, whose patient work helped this first-time author realize the dream of producing a book of my work.

A word of thanks to my literary agent, William Clark, for your kind representation; to Madge Baird at Gibbs Smith for shepherding the process from proposal to print. Gratitude to all the talented photographers who've captured my work so beautifully, and to designers Doug Turshen and David Huang for bringing the book's pages to life.

A heartfelt word of thanks to my family, Lisa, Isabelle, and Charlie.

A debt of gratitude to my friend and business colleague Matteo Scaiola.

And finally, profound thanks to my wonderful clients. Thank you for placing your homes in my hands.

THE AUTHOR

Philip Gorrivan opened his multidisciplinary design firm in New York City in 2001, incorporating interior design, architecture, and product design. Since then, he has become known for stylish interiors that marry elegant historical references with sophisticated modernism. In addition, he has designed collections of fabric, wallpaper, rugs, lighting, and luxury beds. Gorrivan resides in Manhattan and keeps a country home in Connecticut's bucolic Litchfield Hills.

I envisioned a fresh take on tropical style, influenced by the Italian Modernist movement, for the 2022 Kips Bay Decorator Show House. The sitting room I designed (see page 5) featured an adjacent terrace (opposite). Artist David Paul Kay painted the floor and stucco surround in a stylized foliage pattern that complements the lush surrounding.

PHOTOGRAPHY CREDITS

Brian Doben Photography, pages 67, 68–9, 70–1, 72–3, 74, 76–7

Miki Duisterhof, page 8

Pieter Estersohn, pages 29, 30–1, 32–3, 34–5, 36, 37, 38–9, 41, 42–3

Philip Gorrivan, pages 94–5 (bottom left), 104, 105, 175 (bottom left), 222

Graydon Herriott, pages 79, 81, 82, 83, 84–5, 86, 87, 88, 89

Maura McEvoy Photography, pages 168, 170–1, 172–3, 174 (upper left, upper right, middle right, bottom right, bottom middle), 176–7, 178–9, 180, 181, 182, 183, 184, 185, 186, 187, 188, 189, 190–91

Joshua McHugh, pages 15, 16–17, 19, 20–1, 22, 23, 24–5, 26–7, 52, 54–5, 56–7, 58, 59, 60–1, 62, 63, 64, 65, 106, 108–9, 110, 111, 112, 113, 114, 115, 128–9, 130, 132–3, 134–5, 136, 137, 138–9, 141, 142–3, 144–5, 146–7, 148, 149, 150–1, 153, 154, 155, 156–7, 158–9, 160, 161, 162–3, 164, 165, 166–7, 193, 194–5, 196, 197, 198, 199, 200–1, 202–3, 204–5, 206–7, 208, 209, 210, 211, 212–13

Image Copyright Read McKendree/JBSA, pages 2, 45, 46–7, 48, 49, 50–1, 215, 216, 217, 218–19, 220–1

Valery Rizzo, pages 12–13

Nick Sargent Photography, pages 5, 223

Simon Upton/Interior Archive, pages 91, 92–3, 94–5 (upper left, upper right, bottom right), 96–7, 98–9, 100, 101, 102–3

© William Waldron/OTTO, pages: 117, 118–19, 120, 121, 112–23, 124–25, 126, 127

First Edition
28 27 26 25 24   5 4 3 2 1

Text © 2024 Philip Gorrivan

End papers: *Desert Storm Thistle*, a design by Philip Gorrivan

Published by
Gibbs Smith
P.O. Box 667
Layton, Utah 84041

1.800.835.4993 orders
www.gibbs-smith.com

Designed by Doug Turshen and David Huang
Printed and bound in China

Gibbs Smith books are printed on either recycled, 100% post-consumer waste, FSC-certified papers or on paper produced from sustainable PEFC-certified forest/controlled wood source. Learn more at www.pefc.org.

Library of Congress Control Number: 2023942680
ISBN: 978-1-4236-6494-9

Printed in China using FSC® Certified materials

MIX
Paper from responsible sources
FSC® C153458
www.fsc.org